Sadness & Sadness Accessories

poems by

AURORA HATCHEL

*To Little Aurora, these are the sadnesses you
endured and the lessons they taught me.
It was never a fair exchange,
you beautiful warrior.*

table of poems

i'll never kill myself but—

The Abyss I stare into are the eyes
Of a beautiful woman made of ink.
She is clothed in starlight, each motion
Forming constellations and supernovae,
And yes, Neitzsche, she stares back into me.
Each eye is a pool I can dangle my feet over
And think about what it would be
To fall into her.

I do not want to go back home to my Father,
The God, the parent, and the pastors who have offered me
Whip after whip to divine my flesh.
They are all trying to find the cancer in me
And free me from it with brute force.

But the Abyss speaks my language of absolutes
My wickedness is not one seed.
The whole field is salted and barren.
And she will not settle for half my soul
Or a slice of my limping life.
She wants all of me,
And with a hand on my cheek,
And kisses like velvet on my chapped lips,

She tells me I will never have to look from her again,
And she will gaze into my eyes forever.

As though my eyes hold the infinite like an abyss
When in fact, they only hold the splendor of her reflection.

Some days I wonder if I will feel regret
If I were to kiss her back.
Would the nothingness of death have room for it?
All the things I failed to do.
The tiny hands I'll leave behind.
They may hate me, but I'll never know.
They may miss me, but I won't feel the guilt of failing them.
The Abyss and I will sleep in each other's arms
With the blacked out night of a sunless earth
Pulled snugly over our oblivion.

But there won't be warmth
Or kisses,
And I need to know who Ruthie will be
Because she is always budding like fireworks,
And Giddy will write such stories
That I know they will reach me in eternal nothingness.

Judah will rescue an entire world
And be dissatisfied because I am still not there.

And Esther?
She simply won't have any of it.
She is like my Becah, who will rip me
From the arms of my siren lover,
And in her eyes, show me another abyss,
A blue sky falling up in all directions
Over a flat and endless Kansas plain.

And when that light stares back into me
I always find a way to step back
To curl against a tree and anchor myself
While the Abyss weeps for want of me.

how to write a poem

The first poem was an accident
The cut was puffy and dripped
On the page, shallow and fresh.
It had some metaphor about lesbians,
So I kept cutting diligently.
Remove the epidermis, let it heal.
Pick the scab and show it to your friends,
Disgusted concern for the boy playing poet.
The poems had to go deeper.
Hide in the bathroom so they run
Wet and thick down porcelain white,
Stain the carpet and your crooked teeth,
Find the muscle and tear.
Do not scream, not yet,
The fibrous meat is tasty.
It sells like pornography, this pity,
This gasp at the start of your freak,
Show them scars, your collection,
Publications in the mirror,
Competitions want another submission.
Submit another.
Submit the pound of flesh.

Dig to the bone, find a rusty saw,
Something to bite down on,
Scream now.
The dust of your ribs is salty,
Brining the blood, tossing copper
On the wind, fill your lungs,
And tear until you feel the cracks,
Until you have a mess.
Then you have a poem.

book wyrm

When It comes for me:
Give me a closet to withdraw in.
Give me a pink candle that glows
On yellow pages in my hands.
If I lean forward too much,
The words will wash me away.
The tide of fairy tales will lure me out
Until my closet is a beached landmark
For pirates and poets to sail by.

a rejection letter for jk rowling

Dear Joanne,

I am writing to inform you
That your application
To the Badass School of Queer Witches, Wizards,
and Warlocks
Has been denied.

This, of course, has everything to do with
Your fear of magic.
Joanne, we at the Badass School of Queer Witches, Wizards,
and Warlocks
Have never met a muggle with such
A crippling lack of imagination.
In your world riddled with
Forced Latin translation –
As though Magic resided only in the Catholic Church –
You have created nothing more
Than a foggy reflection of this world
Crammed with whimsical names.

You had the opportunity to make
The world anyway you wanted

Yet you decided to include:
Racism, white supremacy, and ethnic cleansing.
This simply will not do, Joanne.
It is an abhorrent misuse of
The oldest school of magic: stories.

We at BSQWWW are not insensitive
To your plight, Joanne.
You have forced yourself to live
In a narrow field of vision
And a mundane world.
At our institution, we value inspiration, novelty, and color
Too much to ever invite you to dim our doorstep.

We have seen your attempts to publish under pen names.
You are asking yourself if it was a fluke.
Maybe you have no talent.
Maybe the global phenomenon of Harry Potter
Had more to do with the wishful thinking of abused and
lonely children
Than your words or derivative Christ narrative.

It is a shame you have so thoroughly rejected
The trans community.

We are experts at dispelling the curse of Imposter Syndrome,
Just as we are Divine Truth Tellers.
We could have told you that, in fact,
Your success was indeed a fluke
And the world no longer needs your writing
Burdened with contradictions and stereotypes.

Among the various misuses of magic in your application,
We would like to address some of the more egregious offenses
So that you may know exactly why you aren't welcome here.

Our admissions officers were baffled that you created
A world with Polyjuice potion and no trans characters.
Honestly – and this is not a rhetorical question
– are you stupid?
Talk about a missed opportunity.
What trans girl wouldn't stew lacewings
For weeks on end to feel feminine for an hour
In safe and authentic anonymity?

Additionally, your magic recks of fear.
Especially of bathrooms.
In your world, the Gryffindor staircase protects
The girls' bathroom from boys

No matter the enchantment they use
But the boys' bathroom requires no such defensive wards.
Joanne, we're not just disappointed; we're mad.

It is as though you are the Dark Lady,
Trapping minorities in a cruel and cursed book
Where they are told their tropes are reality
And then you gave that damned book to children.

That is your crime, Joanne.
You made a little girl believe in magic
And then you used your platform
To do your best to take it away from her,
Like we are filthy mud-bloods.

But our magic isn't in the letters that never came
Or the wand, you phallic obsessed bigot.

Our magic is in the shots of T and pills of E
Like Polyjuice potion that lasts.
It's in a room of requirement that fills the whole world,
In pronouns, expression, being treated with dignity,
Casting a spell that builds yourself,
And using the right fucking bathroom.

And we at the BSQWWW never had to make it up
Or sell a lie to children so we could become billionaires
Or cozy up to misogynists and transphobes
to make ourselves feel big.
Our magic was in us the whole time,
And you clearly have none of it in you.

a letter to my body from the frontline

Beloved,

I don't know how to stop this war
Between us.
My life has always felt like a dream
In media res:
Key plot points missing,
Characters acting erratically,
No motivation, no narrative arc.
Just forward.
But always, there has been our war.

Did it start with my penis forming in the womb?
Why did you do that to me?
I swear, no ambassador you send
Will ever help me understand
That first betrayal.
You strangled
My one wild and precious life
Before I had the chance
To properly fuck it up myself.

Or maybe it was when we discovered

The crippling crisp sweetness of Mountain Dew.

Though the photos exist, I cannot remember

A time without the rolls lining my stomach

Like decadent pastries stuffed with cinnamon and butter.

Dear God, butter is almost as culpable as you.

And because of your disgusting stomach

I have hidden my body a dozen different ways.

Pizza has sat with me in the trenches

Though I know he fights for both sides.

He has been such a balm to my soul,

That I forgive him his treachery.

After all, it is you that craves him

Even if it is me that orders him to my bedside.

He leaves me bloated like a corpse

Left in a muddy river for maggots,

And yet, as soon as he is gone,

I thank him and ache for his touch again.

Body,
I cannot put down my gun.
Even if you surrender today,
I will stay in this trench until the end,
Keeping watch,
Ready for the moment you show
Your flabby and weak self again.
Or one of your fucking allies:
Asthma with the bright red face,
Beard with skin covered in course needles,
Penis, erect and embarrassing.
And if I name them all, I'll lose myself
To rage.

It doesn't matter how much I heal,
No therapist follows me to the mirror
And watches my clothes stretch tight
Or has to pass by thigh-high boots
That will never fit your size sixteen feet.

Know that I am tired,
But I will not relent.
In the end you will be dust,
And I will still have my weapon trained on you.
Less some theologies are right
And I am cursed to wear you forever
While you tarnish even heaven for me
As you have made a hell for me here.

And also, I'm sorry.
I don't know how not to hate you.
No matter how much I wish I could.
You were like a daughter to me
That I could never quite understand.
You deserve better.
And so do I.

I'll see you across the trench tomorrow,
Sincerely,
Ego

to the beauty in the mirror

My God,
You are lovely,
Soft and pale,
Curved and bright.
Your tummy must be
Formed from the foam
Of an ancient sea.

I want to drape
Your smooth skin
With kisses.
Sweet goddess,
There is so much of it.
Like a gift of Elysium.
Yes, even the scars
Like stitches holding
A masterpiece together

rivers like ribbons

The river in New Orleans is not
The same river slicing through Memphis.
Here it trades a rushing green
For a swirling brown. It flows
Backwards and forwards in the same spot.
So it is with me. The same blue
Eyes but new skin. All this death
Flaking off of me. The return.
The echo. Ghosts in the ultrasound.
A murmur, not a spasm. The gossip
Of what could be if we do not cease
The whispering.

In one river I am drowned. Levies
Become lies become bridges. A man sits
Beside me, he is who I used to be.
His feathers molt and children gather them
Like shells at the Gulf, the sewers
Sweeping away both Memphis and New Orleans.

My shadow, myself, my aspiration.
We will come, one drunk trio, spilling
Onto the shores. There I hope to stand,
Arms spread wide, greeting old friends.
I have chartered a boat for us.
The ferryman will take us to the Jordan.
Pennies in our eyes, the pyre burning bright.

what kind of day it has been

I find myself blaming everything on the Capitalist Pigs lately.
Even the kind of mother I am.
One out of every ten Americans take antidepressants,
and we're one of two counties in the world that allow
public advertisements for prescription drugs

The ones with fit housewives looking longingly
at their children playing outside
like the window is a television showing
a documentary of her family.
In the second act,
her shirt shows more cleavage and
she's hanging off her husband's arm
as he grills dead animal.

It's a good ad. Sells product. Investors love it.

I think about the Capitalist Pigs because
Someone should tell them they're winning.
I'd like to shake the hand of the CEO
of Diagnosing and Prescribing Sadness
and Sadness Accessories.
He should know he's a pioneer in the industry.
He's revolutionizing profit margins.

Just like everyone else,

I never wanted to make a lot of money.

Just enough money.

Enough for clothes and food and

healthcare for my sad pills and a house

- okay, a nice house.

Maybe some vacation time and money to travel.

But I never needed a yacht for Chrissake.

When you become a public school teacher,

you're not in it for the money.

No matter how many bonuses they offer me for performance

- like I'm a call girl of grammar putting in the extra work

for tips.

Like I won't give my students the secrets

of sentence diagramming

unless the superintendent tosses me a few extra grand.

One of my mentor teachers told me about ending

each day of work with a trip to 7/11.

He'd get a Big Gulp filled three quarters with Diet Coke,

then go home and fill the rest with Jack Daniels.

I wonder why I don't see more ads with dead-eyed teachers,
their room in chaos as kids hit each other like their parents
hit them.
But then they drink a glass of Jack Daniels
and they've got great cleavage and the kids sit in tidy rows
writing essays about the National Anthem
as though it isn't a song celebrating the beauty
of a bombing.

I used to sneak out of my room at night
and finish off the half-filled glasses by the sink.
Partly because I was anxious about our water bill,
but partly because we weren't allowed soda
and the dark liquid of my father's Diet Coke called to me.
It didn't taste like soda but a punch in the throat,
like my father was a dragon putting out the fire in his chest
with flowing amber.

I try to convince my students that there's an industry
for everything.
When I ask them what they want to be,
they give me the stock photo answers:

lawyer, fireman, marine, police officer, nurse, businesswoman.
But there is a job for everything.
There is a therapist that works at Betterhelp.com
and there is an entrepreneur behind them
who sees wellness as a business,
who is investing in our hope for health.
For a small fee, of course.

Growing up, my father's arrival home was
THE event of the day.
Whether for grim or glory, the house itself would
hold its breath for the moment he walked in.
The oven would slow itself down to
make sure his food was hot,
I swear to god.

It wasn't until I started shuffling home at six
to four pairs of beaming eyes
that I understood my bitterness:
My god was just a man worn weary by a job
He could not leave because we needed money.
Not a lot of money.
Enough money.

So this god gone ghost went straight for his recliner
and his perpetual glass of Diet Coke.

I wanted to work in a school that needed me most.
The best teachers should be in the toughest schools
like the best bodybuilders lift the heaviest weights.
And I spent all day hustling to these students
the classic spiel about working hard and defying the statistics,
like they didn't have their parents' genes,
like I'm not burning up right along with them,
on both ends, hoping my good deeds keep me
out of the sadness industry,
or worse, the alcohol industry
- a subsidiary of the great Sadness Industrial complex.

Some nights,
I can't move once I sit down at the end of the day.
My toddlers crawl all over me
and ask me what's wrong or tell me to wake up.
But their play is like a documentary of some other family,
like the ad for anti-depressants I can't afford,
and I wonder if my father felt the same way.

Did he watch my life like some hidden producer
wondering if he got his money's worth?
Is this the film he envisioned
when he was still storyboarding me in the womb?

One son kisses me when I'm lost like this.
He does it to wake me because this is a fairytale,
and I am under some curse.
Some big Bad Capitalist Pig told me
what it takes to buy the blockbuster life
I want for my children.
No matter the hours.
No matter the Diet Coke sweating in my hand,
this potion eating me up,
keeping me going, and
staying affordable to boot.

I have internalized that
I am only the things I get done.
And worse,
I am especially the things I don't get done.

The work following me home
in emails
and planning
and grading.
I am
the stories I don't read to my boys and
the games I'm too tired to play with my girls.

So when my oldest asks me how work was,
I barely lift my head
because work isn't over.
The pipes need to be looked at and
the fridge is busted and
somewhere in this goddamn house
there has to be a Diet Coke.

drinking with my brother

Tonight I am floating

My feet touch the ground

Like existential ennui

And philosophy drips from my lips

Wine and epistemology

Each thought is easy

Words precede meaning

Persuasion is a con

So there is only talking

Each word, once sharp,

Now soft and escaping

Before I can think

I am relating too simply

Like fire to gasoline

ineffable

At first there were words
Un-tongued and burning from
Within. But not burning.
Before burning and words like burning,
There were words perched
On the heavens unspoken:
Pre-perch and pre-heaven.
Words dwelling with God,
Words making up God, not as some,
Linguistic theology of abstract nouns
Requiring concrete wordiness,
Needing paper flesh and inky veins,
No, the words are God
In that God is the words,
An unbroken tango gliding
Throughout the pre-stars in pre-dance.

But being am who am and stirring
The volatile soup of verbiage to be
Spilling out of itself onto a
Blank, pre-blank, canvas,
Igniting the very idea of ignition
So that beginnings, as the first beginning,
Reverberate over the skin,
Goosebumps of Deep Magic from
Before Time, of creation shouting
In hoarse whispers:
"Finally beginning has begun,
To begin in the beginning and will begin,
Began, and forever will beganning. Amen"

mom, this one is about you

Mother,
Thank you for being my South Star,
For illuminating all the paths I shouldn't take,
For letting me know if my compass was broken
Because only damaged things point to you.

And yes, this poem is actually about you.
It's not a metaphor for the Mother Earth
That held me in her dark arms
when you slapped me to the ground.
I'm not speaking about Mother God
Or the great Feminine Divine
That welcomed me with kisses
When you wanted a dissertation
Before you'd accept my identity.
But ambiguity is the shield of cowards,
So let me be clear,
This one is about you, bitch.
Let me hold your face up to the sun
And have posterity judge you
If your vampire skin docsn't turn to dust first.

When I was fourteen, I tried to kill myself
In the dark, where I was safe from you.
When I failed, you denied me therapy
So that I wouldn't talk shit about you,
All while you reminded me each morning
That I was a burden you could barely afford.

The worst is that I can never escape you.
Like Annie Wilks, you have broken the legs
Of my mind, giving my thoughts a limp.
You thought to keep me forever,
But I have sawed off my legs at the thigh
To crawl away from the solitary confinement
You called a home.

This poem will be the last people hear of you.
Instead of forgiving, I will forget you.
Shake the dust from my broken bones,
And the drafty corners of my wounded heart.
For now I know how hard it is to be a mother,
But it's never as hard as you made it out to be

maty's day

Maty is Ukrainian for mother.
And when my babushka slapped me
For putting a drink on the coffee table
Without a coaster,
She slapped the orthodox culture into me.
Orthodox like a family: Mother and Father.
Or the Trinity without femininity soiling their sanctity.

I chose to be called Maty when I became unorthodox,
When Daddy cut me like a kiss covered in barbed wire.
My wife loved that it still sounded like Daddy,
To make it easier for the kids, of course,
But harder for me.
We became Maty and Momma,
Or sometimes they called her Mommy,
Or Mom.
Something orthodox.

On Mother's Day, JK Rowling,
Whose books my wife and children love,
Tweeted a celebration of all birth giving parents,
As if spitting on millions of adopted mothers
Is worth it to her if some stray spittle lands on my face.

In my house, we made a new holiday – Maty's Day.
Not on Mother's Day, not on my birthday.
It was a day of stumbling words and good intentions.
My children don't know about a uterus or my lack of one.
They know my snuggles, my deep voice, my kisses.
They know Maty. Rhymes with Daddy.

When I tuck Little Aurora in at night
And tell her all the things no one told Little Robert,
I don't feel like a second-class mother.
Like the mom we have at home, the off-brand Mommy.
But how many years must I hold my children
In my weary arms
Before I can say I carried them inside of me?

Little Aurora has no answers.
She looks at me with her big blue eyes
And we sit in silent motherlessness.
Her maty without a womb, my mom without a heart.

The only child I carry in me is an eternal maybe.
Maybe I was meant to be this way; maybe I'm Mom.
And on my best days, I can push it to an almost.
Maty's Day is almost Mother's Day.
And though almost suggests a crack in the door,
When I look into Little Aurora's eyes,
There is a chasm of orthodoxy between me and Her.

musth

I

Elephants experience grief
And hold elaborate funeral rites.
They kiss the body with their trunks
One last time on the forehead
Before their beloved joins their mothers
And the herd in an eternal Savannah
Where there are no poachers, no chains.

A herd of elephants is called a memory,
And juvenile bull elephants never forget
As much as they may want to.
In 2002, a gang of orphaned bulls
Rampaged across South Africa.
They killed and raped over sixty-three rhinos,
Endlessly repeating the scene taught to them by
The men who offered their aunts a watermelon
Filled with the flavor of bitter almonds.
She shared it with her memory,
But then they each collapsed from the cyanide.
More men appeared, now with machetes
And they sliced the tendons of their mothers to immobilize them.

They severed the trunks to bleed them quicker.
And then they took their damn ivory.
But they left the children
Chained to their mothers in the heat
And bathed in the stench of corpses
Because the young don't have sufficient ivory
And time will fatten them up for watermelon.
The little ones do not know the funeral rites
For the women in their memory.
The only kiss is from their chains.
Their afterlife is reiterated pain.

After they have poached the sixty-three rhinos,
These juvenile bulls are put down.
Though somewhere else, another gang arose
From the lack of memory.
In Sierra Leone, a village of three hundred,
Was pinned by giant feet as tusks
Slid lovingly into their chests like a kiss,
Like a funeral the body knew
Though the bulls had never seen it before.

II

The only males permitted in a memory
Are the children.
Female elephants are the herd species.
When a male comes of age, an urge to wander
Haunts him, a curse in his bones called Musth.
A rise in temporin and a steady trickle of urine
Down his leg is an indicator
That he is in Musth.
He is overcome with the restless ache
To leave his sisters, mothers, and aunts,
To spread the rich scent of himself over the plains,
To find a mate and impregnate her
Until the Musth drives him away from her memory.

Musth makes the bull too dangerous to stay.
He becomes violent and territorial,
And to heal this, he spends weeks alone,
Lumbering towards the horizon,
Connecting the dots of his mother and mate
With a trail of piss down his legs.
None of his brothers go with them,
Like lions, the son is a threat to the father,

And only women are fit for family.
The bull is made for self-reliance
And slow but determined marches toward
the western flatlands.

Musth is considered healthy in the adult male,
Even as it makes him irritable and aggressive
As he sees his own brother as a threat
As his mother says he is too strong to stay home,
Too virile to be left alone with his sisters,
Too fearless to watch over his grandmothers.

An elephant song is like the rumble of the earth,
A groan from the ancestors across time and hurt.
Elephant songs are too deep for human ears
But carry up to six miles away so that
They can always reach out to the memory.
Musth makes the bull oversensitive to sound
So the same song his sister hummed
To bring him home each night
Now drives him further away.
It Musth.

III

In the book, *Detransition, Baby,*
A character compares trans women
To juvenile elephants,
A generation of traumatized children
Trying to raise themselves
When the only memory they have is pain.

But the bulls would never have a memory.
Even in a perfect world
With no AK-47s filling the buzzing African air,
Drowning out the barely audible hum
Of mothers calling out to daughters
Like earthquakes call out to mountains
Begging them to return return return.

In this imaginary and flawless world,
The bull would follow his dick.
The need for a womb to fill
Turns him from a member of the memory
To a predator that kisses no brother
On the floppy ear before he goes.
He would simply charge towards pussy

Because he Musth.

Without the poachers, the juvenile bull
Would not be trapped in a cave where
Pain calls out to pain in waning echoes.
But that would leave him to the Musth,
Where each generation is washed away
With the inevitable kiss of a wave,
And the son reinvents himself
As the father he imagines having
Rather than the father who abandoned him.

IV

Some of my trans brothers describe
The psycho-emotional effects of testosterone
On their sex drive
Like Dr. Jeckyll's magic formula
Turning them into monsters
Who want to claim a territory
That they can't properly define.

One friend said he feels like a rapist
Whenever women bend over and fantasies
Of cruelly taking them fill his mind.
It is the hunger that scares him,
That makes every male a competitor,
Even the married and chaste.
From morning wood to wet dreams,
Every cell in his body Musth.

From the lonely Savannahs of football fields,
Or the chained weights of the gym,
To the father he can't stand,
He Musth walk into a horizon,
The lone wolf action hero as a mentor,

And the memory of all the terrible things
That happened to his mother,
The memory he wanders further and further away from.
Because he Musth.

V

When Torrey Peters says I am a juvenile elephant
Chained to the corpse of the person I used to be,
I do not think she knows
There were never going to be parents
Whispering truth to me.
My mother would be lost to a memory,
And my father lost in the wilds,
Killing off his neighbors.
Because he Musth.

I raised myself without a memory,
Dragging the corpse of my family around,
With no songs to guide me home or away,
And only the testosterone raging in me,
Pissing myself as I stumbled through the world,
Panicked erections waking me up
In the middle of the lonely nights,
Hair sprouting from my everywhere,
And only the Musth gave me any direction.

Away.

VI

I want Torrey Peters to know that
I am not a juvenile elephant
Anymore.
As my brothers laid waste and made war,
I went to the graves of my memory,
And begged them to teach me
How to family,
Because I'd rather lose my trunk,
And my precious ivory,
I'd rather eat watermelon,
And be chained to their corpses,
Than be forced away from my sisters.
Because I couldn't take another lonely day,
Wandering away from my own corpse,
Temporin raging through my body,
Showing me how to rip and ravage,
Turning me against sister and stranger alike,
Tearing the song from my chest
That has haunted me everyday since
The sky opened up and hot lead
Rained through me like razor blades.

I do not know how to kiss the dead like my mothers
Or carry my lost children in our funeral rites
Because I was once cursed to be male
And an elephant never forgets
Even when she has no memory of how to grieve,
Though somehow, I must.

femininity

For a trans woman, I overly struggle
With spelling the word femininity.
You see, I never expected all the eyes
In a feminity I was not native to.
F-E-M-Eye-N-Eye-N-Eye-T-Y.

It's an eye opener to see feminism struggle with me
Because every inch of shaved skin I crave
Is a step back from the hairy legs they fought and died for,
So I'm battling with my heroes online with all our eyes
on feminity.

Eye on the prize with transition timelines,
So feminity can be a destination.
And then it's over. And I have it.
Is there anything more feminine than that naivety?

Eye for an eye when she misgenders me
and I call her ugly, making me more so,
Because maybe ugly is the closest a cis woman
Can get to wearing feminity like me.

Keeping one eye open when I walk into a bathroom
Because in there it doesn't matter if I see myself as a woman.
Only mirrors matter in there and the ones our mothers gave us,
Sewing them into our eyes.

My wandering eye that scans over each lovely
Trans person, trying to reassemble their assigned gender.
The hypocrisy is not lost on me. Forgive me.
It's just the woman inside of me, the catty cunt
Who is constantly preparing her insulting comeback

The Stars in my eyes. The ones whose pictures
I tape up on the wall like they're my only family left,
The bodies I will never have no matter what I pay science
to do to me.
These shoulders I can't hide. These hips I can't make.
The little matter of bones that don't give a fuck about
how I identify.

And to everyone I see, I am sorry
For my eye getting in your feminity.
I'm trying to find the right box for you.
Butch or femme. Amab or enby.

I am still unlearning toxic feminity
Because when you're drowning, you don't care
How polluted the air is when you break the surface.
So we all spell the word wrong
And let spell check tell us it needs more eyes
And slowly let it pull us back to our lonely depths.

queer haikus

I.

Everything I do
Is what a woman would do
Because I am a

Woman

II.

All I can manage is quiet
Hovering over my pieces
No 'and' in sight

III.

A body is not
A haunted or lost wreckage
No matter the scars

Or cruel reflections.
Of mirrors we fucking smashed
Cut ourselves upon

A body is an
Aftermath, a sweet story
Rich in fond sadness

Let your body be
A trusted god's lost temple
A beloved ruin

IV.

I write poems so that
Emily Dickinson will
Kiss me in heaven

in my flashbacks, we are all ghosts

"If I say, 'surely the darkness will hide me
and the light become night around me,'
even the darkness will not be dark to you;
the night will shine like the day,
for darkness is as light to you."
  – Psalm 139: 11-12

6
Under the bed it's hot.
The air is thick with my sweat
Each breath is held and punctuated.
No one has found me
It took ten seconds to disappear,
Four hours to find me.
I am involuntarily camouflaged.

  14
I moved to the closet.
No one noticed.
I am curled with a book;
Perks of Being a Wallflower first,
Catcher in the Rye second.

I am listening to "Iris."
No one tells me to turn it down.
They cannot hear my song.

19

Catching my breath in a coat room.
Outside, five thousand Christians worship
In deep V-necks and skinny jeans.
When I could not stand their eyes,
I found Narnia beyond the walls.
I don't remember it being so dark.
Or the spiders.
Or the hands.

20

Dear God, the hands.
They are in sprawling shadows,
Just left off greasy streets.
In the cold fog they taste me.
No one sees the tongues clawing me.
They've all stopped looking.
I am still beneath the bed.

Count to ten.

I want to reappear.

It's all a mean trick. Aren't I funny?

You were supposed to keep looking

Don't you see?

How can you not see?

The blood pooling outside the door?

Open it up, I'm begging you.

Don't leave me with Holden, with Charlie,

With whispers breathing down my neck.

Aren't I funny?

Aren't I funny?

Aren't I funny?

conversations with sleeping people

I'm sorry
When I said I felt like you were holding me hostage,
I meant that you were the hostage negotiator
And my mother held her pistol to my temple,
Arm around my throat, the way she loved to hug me.
I can feel the cold metal against the bone,
And when you beg someone to drop the weapon,
I don't know which one of us you're talking to.

Sorry.
And sorry for saying sorry like people say 'um.'
It's not the word I'm looking for.
You see, English is my second language,
And Sorry is my native tongue,
Taught to me by touch like knives.
It translates roughly to "stop," to "please
Let me haunt these halls if being a ghost means
I'll get to live without the body we all hate."

Sorry. It's all getting so heavy now.

I have to go before the waters of quiet
Rise above the sea level of our bed
And carry us out across the great Melancholia.

I know you think I'm quiet,
But there is a deeper quiet, like the one from under a bed
When you play competitive hide and seek
But it's not for fun.
Despite all its rehearsals, it's a game with live ammo,
And the sound of your breath
Might as well be an airplane engine
Because there is something moving in the house:
Footsteps of parents become strangers.
My chest tries to crawl under the floorboards
Like some Tell-Tale Heart, and I am with
the Cask of Amontillado,
I am both Montresor and Fortunato,
I am sinking into the stillness, listening for the Raven,
The rapping, tapping on my childhood door,
Quoth the Raven, "Sorry."

when i heard the learn'd linguist

The Wrath of my wife speaks French.
The fingers grind fricatives but her
Lips leave silent morphemes for me to deduce.

But when she wants me,
Her hips know only her native German.
I hear my heart glottal stop when she purrs.

Last night she fell asleep naked
With only the moonlight from an open window
To give her dreams language.
The murky blue room glows silver and
The constellations on her back translate:
I am, I am, I am.

my voice

Can you hear my voice?
Is my voice, the voice you are hearing?
My voice which fills this room
And sometimes still doesn't have room for me.

This voice belongs to my my feminine job
Of herding a classroom of middle schoolers.
It is booming like my father's,
Crafted like Zeus's thunderbolts,
Made to scare children and dogs.
So we all scamper under my bed,
And we cry
Because one day we will be storm giants ourselves,
Covered in hair and
Terrifying the masses.

And when I speak like a mother
To my children, holding back the giants in the sky,
I tell them they're safe, a cozy lie.
It is my voice, not my words, that soothes them.

It is my voice that gets quieter
When I go out in public
So it matches my dress.

It is my voice that tells the dog to
Stop pissing on the rug!
It is my voice that whispers
To my lover and tells her
That I am always the same.
I am always one voice
Lost under all these other voices.

My voice sounds the same on every piece of paper
And that's the way I like it best.
But to live a full life as myself,
I have become an obsessive scholar,
Activist, and victim of voices -
Pitch and resonance
Breathiness, **chest voice**, *nasal voice*
Cadence, *rhythm, upturn at the end -*
All to make somebody comfortable
Who is not me

god or thunder or Louis

They say my son can hear his father's voice
Best from inside the womb. Something about
Deeper voices penetrating the uterus.
To Judah I am a thunderstorm, or Louis Armstrong,
All brass and bass telling bad Dad-puns.
I may even be the voice of God,
The voice he will forget in all the trauma:
Birth canals, umbilical snips, searing light,
Brighter than twelve Rockefeller Christmas trees
Stinging his soft blue eyes, his fragile everything.
He will think he is dying when he is born.

Squirming boy, one part your mother and one part poetry,
Remember my voice. I sang you show tunes until
I forgot the lyrics. I would pretend I could hear
Your heartbeat and narrate your mother's folding
In the style of radio drama or Casey Kasem.
Remember the nights we couldn't sleep, so we
Planned your arrival like train engineers with maps?
I wish I could spark the memory of our morning chats,
But I am not the voice of God or thunder or Louis.
The only song I can sing for you will be this:
"Remember me? I am your father. I am your father."

waiting

Never before have I been able
To hold a prayer in my arms.
Nine pounds and two ounces, the weight
Of years crying out to the reluctant night.
The weight of her tears drenching
My clothes as I trudge through barren sands.
The weight of two families
Melded behind closed blue eyes.

The wait of Hannah, bedraggled and
Red eyed in her nightgown before Eli.
The wait of a little girl to be a woman
Whose white dress was not enough.
The wait of a woman who could not
Wear a dress at all.

The weight of the wait, long in
Forty-one weeks, short in 21.5 inches,
Small enough to carry and weep,
Too large to fit on this page
Or all the pages to come of the story
He will write.

tiny hats

I'm supposed to say that you were so little,
But you were infinite.
You were fusion and fission,
Kissing and ripping, waves and shore

Now you are eating the dirt.
Everything you eat is older than you.
The applesauce is wiser.
But it cannot break into grins
Or wear tiny hats.
God bless tiny hats

imagine a home

"He settles the barren woman in her home
as a happy mother of children."
      – Psalm 113:9

She could not imagine a home
Without stains:
Markers running through the carpet,
Juice dribbling down the walls.

She could not imagine a home
Without noise:
Cries echoing from the crib,
Laughter bubbling out of the kitchen.

She could not imagine a home
Without touch:
Siblings slapping each other silly,
Cuddles stealing the show from Movie Night.

She could not imagine a home.
Now she doesn't have to.

a joyful noise

The first thing I noticed about my wife,
After how her legs looked in those boots,
Was her volume. Her laughter was
Unfettered, shuddering her chest. Our table
Drew stern looks from conversation invaders,
All jealous of her joyful noise.
Her smile was unrestrained, her eyes unshaded.
She was un-everything I had made myself to be.
I had learned to prefer closets and corners;
I would sing alone in the car but still only
Mouth the words, letting them creep out carefully.

Becah taught me to belt and bellow,
That booming is not the same as blustering,
Because Broadway was in my blood.
She made boisterous beautiful when she
Refused to bind beauty for courtesy.
Ballads have no manners, always butting in,
Building up, and burning down the world.
Because Becah is revealing bigger things.
Nothing in her is withheld from us.
When she laughs, she blooms.
Making all things new starts with making:

Loud and blonde, brilliant and blue,
With her eyes open, something dazzling reflects
Heaven.

what a man does

Lee was over twice my age
When he brought me by my hand
Into his house, best described
As a two story trailer that
Permitted the perfume of a bloated corpse
To still haunt the air like smoke.

My whole mind was pulsing
As he led me into his bedroom.
I felt adrenaline painting my mind
With the static of dread and adventure
Stifling the sound of my heartbeat
Like sirens driving away
                Waning
                        Waning
                                Waning

He sat me down as if he were a waiter
And he'd be right back for my drink order.
I'd probably order vodka if I drank
But I needed soda for the sweetness.
I don't remember him sitting down next to me
Because I was tunneling through the carpet with my eyes.

At some point I recognized the grunting on the TV
As the same purr of the demons in my closet.

I felt a hand grab my jeans roughly,
Like he wanted a fistful of popcorn with the movie,
And my pants shrunk around my hips with fear
As the hand began to scrub them,
As if it were possible to wash away
The last fortification of innocence left.

This is what a man does.
He finds his prey, kills it quick,
And then meticulously takes the time to clean the corpse,
An irony coupled with the loving fondling of tiny organs.

He gripped my wrist.
Not aggressive or forceful, but more akin to
Merlin leading Arthur's hand to Excalibur's golden hilt.
I expected to feel his denim as he felt mine,
But I found the rubbery tingle of my nightmare.
The skin of my arm curled into itself
As if I had reached slowly into a cold shower
And I could not prevent the dreary march into the ice.

This is what a woman does.
She yields to his strength and calloused hands,
As she yields to let him inside her,
And yields to release his spawn into the world.

I didn't know what to do anymore.
So he began to pull off my jeans,
Slowly at first, but he began jerking from frustration.

This is what a man does.
His Y-Chromosome and missing father
Compel him to lead
The cows to the barn to be milked
And his bride into the dimly lit marriage bed.

I follow the melding flesh on the screen
As my hieroglyphic guides into the tomb,
And I find myself falling to my knees
Saying a silent prayer before being devoured.
I felt the water retreat into my eyes in an attempt
To obscure the last picture of my virility.

Because this is what a woman does.
She bows at the altar of a phallic god,
Swallowing the last crumb of pride she has left
After her feet were bound again

                        And again

I don't remember the rest.
And maybe that's what a woman does,
That's the only way she would follow him.
I remember him leaving to clean up.
I begged God to let me cry,
As the generations of women before me.
I hoped the tears would wash away the black tar
I could feel clinging to my once unstained skin.
If I could catch them in my hands
I would rinse my mouth out with melancholy.
And this is what a woman does.

here i am

When I get lost among the great tide of society,
I go to the trees.
I ask the sycamores where I am,
But I do not have a sylvan tongue.
So the spirit of Mary Oliver laughs,
Translating the kindly condescension of my grandmothers.
They summon me to their roots,
Tuck me into the warm and soft soil,
And cradle me as time washes over us
Like rain building and falling from their leaves.
When my ears are submerged in loam,
I hear their song passing from root to root
Like a chain of held hands squeezing morse code
Like the forgotten paths of dendrite to dendrite in my mind.

What is an old thing on our young planet?
Sharks have been in our world longer than trees.
Sex is brand new in the story of the cosmos,
And gender younger than that.
My question is still en-caul, swimming and raw,
But my place is ancient and held in wisdom,
Like the song of the clownfish or sea turtle,
Green and baking on a yellow shore.

I am here, the line of my being

Reaches out to the frogs, butterflies, and bearded dragons.

They welcome me, sending pulses through the ages,

A new song playing the notes of my ancestors.

chain

He laughs at my nervous joke
And spittle flies on the dashboard
Laughter turns to coughing
As he perfumes the car with garlic.
This is my chain, they will say.

He leaves the hotel room abruptly.
The old bones holding his thinning skin
Are not strong like mine. He is tired.
A cigarette dances across his lips
Before he returns to my body.

I stay up till dawn chatting with my toilet.
It says we can't fight nature. It knows best.
Between my legs I am a human wastebasket.
Do not call me anointed. Do not speak of soft skin
Or a smooth face or youth found in fingertips.

The chain, they say, is a genetic destiny.
It crawls through my skin when I am lonely.
Lately, I am alone less. I vomit often.
Despite the prayers burning away my veins,
I am that shriveling cigarette on his lips.

My friends say their chain is a bride.
A woman with round hips,
White dress hugging her chest,
With the beach reflected in her hair.
They laugh and say mine will rent a tux.

Some lovers call me anointed, some - their son.
I am an heir to filth and soiled bed sheets.
Perched in the middle of this foreplay,
Beading down my forehead with sweat is a song.
My grandmother sang it when she buttered waffles.

"Let Thy goodness, like a fetter,
Bind my wandering heart to thee."

burning bridges is easier than fixing them

Things will end
And things are next
And much is past
And I am drowning
In the stream of time
My head dips below
The frigid waters
My lungs, sagging balloons,
Won't carry me up
But I am moving toward
The next thing
And missing the horizon

what Susie Asado prays for

She offers him sweet tea, asks when he will find
A girl, And tells him he why he can't find a girl
All in the same breath. She sits him at the bar
Dripping in May sunlight and talks about Fathers
And what they have to do with brides.
Her skin is folded with each friend she has lost
From her straight words. At night she sharpens them
And places them in the quiver of her tongue.

No one gets to heaven without Jesus and the ones
Who don't like Jesus go to Susie Asado.
After sunset she sips wine till two thirty-seven
And spits fire. Her mind is a volcano of
The unwelcome questions behind church doors.
The pastor goes to the elders and the elders
Go to Susie.

But every Thursday she lays her case
Before God in her garden, drunk and weeping.
She asks about barren wombs, dead husbands,
And why Papua New Guinea is going to hell.
She questions Elisha and Annonias and Saphira.
She lays flowers on a tombstone for the
Amalekites and still prays for Judas.

On Fridays she returns empty but for the mystery,
Makes a new batch of sweet tea, and cries out
For the hope that despite the shattered soul of
The universe, something is straining to hold it
All together with blood, With love,
With the promise of an age to come.

short prayers

When I get older
Unless something happens
Unfortunately it might
We won't know
Until it does
After we retire
Before we pass
Up to the point
When clocks wither
Whether we want
Maybe tomorrow
But not yet
–
But soon
Eventually it will
In our lifetime
Next weekend
Perhaps

prism heart

"You must habit yourself to the dazzle of the light
and to every moment of your life."
— Walt Whitman

Sit beneath the waterfall of light

Spilling over the horizon,

Pouring out from heaven into heaven.

Greet the dazzle of the light

With open arms and wet eyes.

Invite it over for dinner.

Demand it stay the night,

Stay the winter, let it see

The first bulbs of daffodils

In Spring, the blooming and

Wilting of every moment,

Each crisp breath making

Picture frames and

Refrigerator magnets.

Listen for the chant

Against your ribs,

Echoing back to you from

The graves of ancestors:

You Exist. You Exist.
And what are you going
To do about it? This existing.
This night filled with
Conversation and cheap wine,
This story spilling from your guts,
Pooling around your feet,
Scarlet and blue,
Solar systems burning
With the light in your eyes.

Fill tomorrow with nets
To catch all the miracles
You will meet in a crowded hallway,
A check-out line crammed with
The wonders of the world
Made mysterious and potent
By the weight of glory
In their trembling fingertips.
The starlight caught in their hair
Whispers prophecies
From their mother.

Tomorrow is writing a cascade
Of stories and leaving them
In willow trees for you to pluck.
Go now, though your legs are weak.
Open up a restaurant in Santa Fe,
Fall in love, get lost in Montana,
Stare at clouds until you forget to eat,
Until the blue dips into you like jazz.
Dazzle yourself. Give me a kiss, and
I will wrap it in silver linen
And keep it in my pocket.
Open your chest, and show the world
A prism for a heart bending
Old sunsets back, making them new.

except for being male
it was relatively painless
– Styled after Mary Jo Bang

Failure is a proper noun,
Capitalized and blazoned on the page
Of my heart. It is the song of
Not Quite Enough ringing in my ears
On dark mornings, brimming with gray,
All I want is to kick down the doors
And fly into that soggy mass
Because the baby won't stop crying,
Looking into his dead father's eyes,
Waiting for the lights to come back on.
His mother is watching us, her head
Ready to speed-dial a miracle or
Force the painting of the ocean to burst
Through our living room, sun and all,
Washing our feet in new salt,
Setting this couch adrift for higher seas.
But no. There are only three digits
Blinking back to her on her phone
The light behind the screen is fading.

numinous

If I were naked in the desert, what
Would I have lost? Not the heartbeat
Of the world, the pulse riding through
My toes when jazz begins the possession.
The clouds will hold the Sky.
On clear days she will fall into
Your arms and whisper blue secrets.

Strip me of smoke gingerly. With the
Lover's hands that cradled the stars.
Take away the murals in my eyes:
Sidewalks, discotechs, Cosmo,
Libraries, The Supremes, and Sean Connery.
Leave me bare, dressed for Death and
Ivory Halls made for waltzing.

I cannot carry illusions into a graven cairn.
The tomb holds light and silver fire on
Angels' wings. I can only dance through
Cemeteries to the arias in my bones.
Leave me fragile but sipping on creation.
This glory is free and painless, pouring over
My feet like hot sand. Each grain
Was once me. It will be me again.

constellations

The sky is a bitch curled at the feet
Of her master. She has stolen
Each star from the dusk, one by one,
And buried them in my neighbor's yard.
T. calls them ghosts and sprinkles them
Across his home like midnight memories.

The skyline is a hearth gone cold and
The rain begins to take off the city's clothes
Slowly unzipping bridges with kisses.

John Coltrane improvises a gentle solo for his second wife,
But Heartbreak is struggling to keep the candles lit.
She cannot hear the steam of his song rising,
A flower budding inside dumpsters and drunks alike.

The swan song he whistles is emptier
Than the black tar dripping off my fingertips,
Than the tea I left on the counter back home
With Heartbreak waiting up for me in the dark.

watchman

"My soul waits for the Lord
More than watchmen wait for morning,
More than watchmen wait for morning."
    – Psalm 130:6

The cat does not join us in the bedroom.
We share one bed: baby, mom, maty, chihuahua,
But the cat must sleep in the living room,
One wall paned with floor-to-ceiling windows
Where he can hunt the dawn or
Stalk the moon. He is a clumsy hunter,
Tabby and obese, he could not catch a fly
If he wished to kill it.
He will find that celestial fire peeking
Through the night at 5 AM, spills of blue
Taint the canvas of stars, his tail twitches,
Pupils dilate until he has become light first,
Light the heavens must borrow
From a far tabby cat in Memphis,
The gray watchman preying on
A sunrise he knows will come.

trans joy

This one is going to be about trans joy
because I'm tired of being a martyr,
as though I'm only valuable when I'm a lesson
for cis people to learn.

I want less talk about getting caught
when we stole our sisters' dresses,
And more talk about feeling a smooth leg rub
against another smooth leg
for the first time in twenty years.
To know that skin can kiss skin
and be none the worse for it,
that friction isn't needed for connection.

When people say they would do anything
for a Dr. Pepper, *right now,*
We all know they're lying.
They won't give up their job, their family,
their dignity.

Less talk about giving up our dignity
and more about leaving a lipstick stain
on the rim of a cold glass of doctor pepper,
that satisfaction in knowing you have left a mark,

of seeing yourself as indelible
instead of a ghost haunting your own life.

And when lovers say they would do anything for the other,
We know that's only *mostly* true.
We know as Meatloaf once said: "I won't do that."
Have a threesome, do the dishes, give up meat,
Or go to your bigoted mother's house.

Less talk about mothers misgendering us
and more talk about finding
those legendary, perfect-fit jeans that make you look hot
but feel comfy all at once.
The kind of pants they write book series about
and make you feel for the first time a part of a sisterhood.

When I was little, I used to prepare my three wishes
before I even found my genie
And the first one, each and every time, was to be a woman.
The second one was to be hot.
The third was for Poison Ivy to kiss me,
even if it killed me.
Who would care if you died as long as
you died a hot lesbian kissing another hot lesbian?

Less talk about dying, metaphorical and literal,

and more talk about smiling at a child in a grocery store

and not being treated like a predator,

of realizing you've become a soccer mom

with cold orange slices

instead of your soccer father who was banned

from your sister's matches because

he yelled too meanly too often too loudly.

If you had asked me if I wanted to be a woman,

I would have said yes. Hell yes. Fuck yes.

But if you had asked me if I wanted to

Lose my friends, my family, my job, all respect in my field,

to go so broke that my house has no heat in the winter,

and I'm huddling against my tiny children for warmth,

all just to feel these tiny glimmers of trans joy,

I would have said no. Hell no. Fuck no.

And I did. For thirty years, each day was one long 'no.'

But now that I'm here,

now that I'm ready to give the sad but angry speech

that will win some cis man an Academy Award,

now that I am at the quite literal bottom

of the quite literal rock,

I would make these trades again in a heartbeat.

Everything.
Anything.
Not for Dr. Pepper or love.
But for me.
For the real me I've been beating up
and locking in a closet for thirty years.
For her, little Aurora, to see her smile,
to let her have a minute of trans joy?
I'd do it all over again
and in each and every timeline.

Yeah. Let's have more talk about that.

dear little Aurora

It is going to be hard.
Worse than you can imagine.
It will be the scariest story
You've ever read.

But it will be worth it.

You are going to wear
Every kind of dress.
You will feel at peace
With your body.
You will be a mom.

A real mom.

And most importantly,
I will be with you
Through each painful step
That makes us.

the end

What is a life?
A cup of coffee.
The burst of a perfectly
Poached egg.
The primal relief
Of the oak's shade.
The endless landscapes
Of smooth skin
And the hurricanes of hot
Breath that ravage them.
Sunlight so thick and lovely
You can swim through it.

When the world ends
With the soft fluttering
Of a closed book,
The best of these will linger
As a child's kiss
Upon our furrowed brows.

the author

When not exploring a new world with her kids in their weekly roleplaying game or escaping a moody YA book, **Aurora Hatchel** can be found living outside of Washington, DC.

She is a mother of four, wife to the best of wives and women, and works as an editor, educator, and writer while she homeschools her children. Her textual awakening was with *The Perks of Being a Wallflower* and *The Catcher in the Rye*, and she hasn't looked back since. Her works explores the challenges of mental health, gender, and trying to be good in a world that often feels too heavy.

www.ingramcontent.com/pod-product-compliance
Lightning Source LLC
Chambersburg PA
CBHW020351160726
47987CB00022BA/2537